July, 2021

Paul & Rennie

All the best to you:

Enjoy!

Ken MacKenzie

OVER THE RAIL FENCE

LESSONS IN LIFE FROM THE FARM

KEN MACKENZIE
ILLUSTRATED BY MAYA COLEMAN

FriesenPress

Suite 300 - 990 Fort St
Victoria, BC, V8V 3K2
Canada

www.friesenpress.com

Copyright © 2021 by Ken MacKenzie
First Edition — 2021

All rights reserved.

No part of this publication may be reproduced in any form, or by any means, electronic or mechanical, including photocopying, recording, or any information browsing, storage, or retrieval system, without permission in writing from FriesenPress.

ISBN
978-1-03-911252-0 (Hardcover)
978-1-03-911251-3 (Paperback)
978-1-03-911253-7 (eBook)

1. BIOGRAPHY & AUTOBIOGRAPHY, PERSONAL MEMOIRS

Distributed to the trade by The Ingram Book Company

TABLE OF CONTENTS

INTRODUCTION

I am a child of privilege. I was privileged to be born into a rural farm family. I was privileged to be raised on a small, family-owned, mixed farm. I was privileged to run barefoot through the fields as a boy. I was privileged to learn to work hard and earn my way. I was privileged to grow up with my father's parents living on the farm with our family. I was privileged to rise early to do my chores before heading off to school. I was privileged to learn to work first, then play. I was privileged to learn to appreciate the satisfaction of a job well done. I was privileged to witness the stoicism of living with pain. I was privileged to enjoy the wealth of being part of an extended family that worked and played together. I was privileged to eat well from the production of the farm and gardens that we tended. I was privileged to care for animals. I was privileged to learn to appreciate nature and her cycles. I was privileged to observe generosity and integrity in business and relationships.

Clearly, at first blush, living in relatively modest surroundings doesn't seem like privilege. To most people, privilege is defined as ready access to material things, the power of economic status, and a life of comparative ease. It is counterintuitive to think that privilege is not only defined as a 'silver spoon' life. Privilege, for me, is the life lessons learned along the way, the relationships made, and the freedom to experience a full and satisfying life.

In the pages that follow, through stories from my childhood and upbringing, I hope to share the lessons that I learned from my parents and grandparents. I am writing this memoir for my own sake. It is important to me to reflect on the lessons of life, how and where I learned them, how they influenced all aspects of my life, and, in turn, to pass them on to the next and succeeding generations.

My plan is to tell some stories. Through these stories, I hope to share what I learned and relate how these lessons have served me throughout my adult life. As I said earlier, these stories are for me. I need to write these stories so I don't forget them or lose their significance in my life. Some of the stories are funny, some are sad, and some are inspiring, but all of them teach me something useful.

THE FARM

I am the first-born child of Archie and Ruth MacKenzie. Our farm was on the outskirts of the village of Burford, Ontario. In 1949, the year of my birth, Burford was a small but busy village of eight hundred people. Its economy was based on agriculture. It was a village so typical of many small towns in Southern Ontario. A feed store, three banks, a farm equipment shop, a bustling general store, along with the local barber shop, diners, and other small shops lined the main street, which was shaded by magnificent maple trees. Of course, there were no stoplights, people knew everyone, cars were left unlocked, and there were four churches, but no police presence or hospital. There was a small primary school and a high school, whose joint population was 180 students. In short, Burford was a peaceful, friendly, busy village. I cannot envision a better place for a boy to grow up.

Our farm was a fertile, seventy-acre property that was recognized as having some of the best loam soil in the area. John (Jock) MacKenzie, my grandfather, purchased the farm in 1945 from the Arthur Luard family, who had owned the farm for 52 years. He was able to purchase the property at a very low price because people believed that the previous owner had committed suicide. Potential buyers were reluctant to acquire this fertile farm. John named the farm 'Elgar Lane' Nellie Elgar, his wife, whom he had married in 1914. The farm buildings were set well back from the quiet highway running through Burford from the larger centres, Brantford to Woodstock. The laneway was long, some two hundred and fifty yards from the road to the house.

Like most farms, the lane was lined with maples, oak, and elm trees. The property was an inviting farmstead to approach. The farmhouse was a large white clapboard house trimmed in green, with gingerbread decorations in the eaves, and surrounded by large, well-tended lawns and many flowerbeds. The front yard was dominated by a huge elm tree, which had a tire swing hanging from one of its high branches. White painted fences framed the yard. Across the lawn, some one hundred yards away, sat the large red barn. The barn was shaped in a U, reflecting the growth of the farm over the years. I remember a stencil in the east gable end of the main barn that indicated that its construction date was 1883. The main barn housed the dairy herd, while the western side of the U was a pig barn, and the eastern end of the barn was originally a horse barn with hay storage above, along with a set of farm scales. The barn was trimmed with white around the windows and on the corners of the buildings. The roof was metal painted green. It was always kept painted and looked fresh and well maintained. The setting was completed with a number of sheds, a chicken brooder house, and a barn for laying hens. It was one of the largest sets of farm buildings in the area, reflecting the productivity of the land it sat on.

Our farm was a typical mixed general farm. Unlike today, where specialization is the norm, mixed farms were the main kinds of farms in those days. The farm housed a purebred herd of Guernsey dairy cows, where we milked thirty cows. Although the milk produced from the cows was the main source of revenue, the flock of a thousand laying hens and herd of twenty sows supplemented the income stream for the farm.

Horses were a big part of farming in the mid-twentieth century. My grandfather was a gifted horseman, working with the teams of heavy horses on the farm. When I was a very young boy, the transition to tractors was made. Granddad continued to have a deep love for horses. He was often asked to be the judge of the teams of horses at the fairs throughout the province. As kids, we had a pony named Patsy, and we enjoyed riding it and driving a small cart. Grandpa understood progress but often wistfully told stories about the simple enjoyment of working with these majestic animals.

Occasionally we would plant potatoes as a cash crop. A large garden completed the output from the farm. Almost all our food was produced on our own farm. The farm was virtually self-sufficient. My mother and grandmother made jams and jellies, preserved fruit, canned tomatoes, and other vegetables. Storage shelves were always stocked with jars and jars of pickles. Our family never lacked good, wholesome food. As an adult, I still have a deep appreciation for simple, tasty, fresh food.

MY FAMILY

I lived on Elgar Lane Farm from my birth until I went to university and got married. I lived on the farm with my father, Archie; my mother, Ruth; and two brothers, Jim and Murray, who were four and eleven years younger respectively. My dad's parents, John and Nellie MacKenzie, lived with us on the farm. My grandparents lived in the rear portion of our house, while we had the front part. John and Nellie were active in the community and had a significant influence on our lives. Mom and Dad were also community leaders and willingly did their part to support the vibrancy of our village.

John MacKenzie was born in Dundee, Scotland, in 1887. He emigrated to Canada in 1907, arriving alone at the port of Montreal. He became a farm hand in the Brantford, Ontario, region shortly thereafter. He told me that his first job paid six dollars for six months, with as much milk, butter, and flour as he wanted, along with a bunk in the horse barn. Grandpa was known as a hard worker, and he was determined to own his own farm. After his marriage to Nellie, they purchased a small farm in the Burford area, where they started their family. He was an even-tempered, fun-loving man. My recollection of Grandpa was that he was rarely seen without a pipe in his mouth or his Scottish tam on his head. He wore long underwear year-round. You knew that summer was coming when he switched to the summer-weight long underwear. He was a powerfully built, strong, stocky man who seemed to always be the first one on the job of attending to farm chores. John was highly regarded in the community. He was known as a man of his word. A handshake from John was as good as his signature. He was a shrewd, but fair businessman who never went back on an agreement. Although he was quiet and stoic, he was at the same time quick with a witty remark. All his grandchildren knew that he loved each one of us. He promised each one of us a gift of two hundred dollars if we did not smoke cigarettes or a pipe until we were eighteen years old. To the best of my knowledge, everyone received that gift. I know that I did. A day did not go by where I did not have an interaction with Grandpa MacKenzie, and to this day, he is often brought to my mind, with his practical words of wisdom ringing in my ears.

Grandma MacKenzie was a tiny woman, born in 1884 in Norfolk, England. She came to Canada, arriving in Quebec City, in 1909. She worked as a housekeeper on the adjoining farm to the farm that my grandfather worked on. Soon, love was in the air. Grandma and Grandpa never shared many details of their courtship, but I know they were married in 1912. Grandma came across as a grumpy, angry woman by her demeanour, and we grandkids trod cautiously around her. However, her actions refuted that impression. She worked hard alongside Grandpa, ran an efficient household, and never complained about any of her circumstances. She had a kind streak and willingly shared with those in need. She could effortlessly prepare a big meal for whoever showed up at the farm, whether it was cousins, surprise visitors, or contract workers.

My dad, Archie, was the youngest of three boys. He had a twin sister, Clair, who lived in Brantford with her husband Tom, and three of my cousins. Dad contracted polio in his early twenties. I never knew him any other way than a man who lived with the effects of this debilitating disease. Dad was a quiet, loyal, calm man. He was often heard saying, "Better to keep your mouth shut and appear a fool than open it and remove all doubt." When he did speak, he showed the depth of his wisdom. He served on various boards and committees in the community. Dad was physically a very strong man, even though his left side was withered from the effects of polio. To compensate, Dad's right side was exceedingly powerful. He routinely tossed sixty-pound bales of hay with one hand more easily than most able-bodied men. Dad and Grandpa Mackenzie farmed together on our farm in a harmonious way. Any strong disagreements were rare. Differences of opinion were objectively dealt with, usually in a few short, direct sentences. Dad stayed up to date with the latest farm technologies, innovations, and news. All these ideas were always put through the filter of what was best for the farm, the livestock, the land, and for our family. His example in this area stays with me today.

Dad had a deep devotion to Ruth, his wife. They made a good team. Mom was a city girl who was ten years younger than Dad. Mom had two siblings—Marion, who lived in Brantford, and Roy, who lived and worked in Sudbury. Mom and Dad met and fell in love at a church social event. Mom made the difficult transition to becoming a farm wife with very few hiccups. She was a good helper to Dad, whether it was with farm chore support, helping him with his health issues, or hosting guests. Where Dad was quiet, Mom was more verbal and welcoming to visitors. She regularly made three pies when company was coming because, "You never know what people will prefer." Mom stood quietly beside Dad in the business world but had a strong understanding of finance. Her insights were invited and heeded by both Dad and Grandpa. Mom was also very pretty. She was won the 'dairy princess' competition at Toronto's Royal Agricultural Winter Fair, which was big news in our local weekly newspaper in Burford. Although she was a city girl, Mom grew to love farm life and her home. She fully embraced her life with my dad on Elgar Lane Farm. I knew they were deeply in love and fully committed to each other.

Dad's older brothers, Don and Bill, owned farms nearby. Both farms were purebred dairy farms. Dad and his brothers shared the use of farm equipment and took turns helping each other as needed. Uncle Don and Uncle Bill married women who were sisters. They each had four children. We kids worked and played together a lot. My four cousins on my mom's side of the family often visited the farm on weekends, usually Sundays. Our farm was often the place where our extended family gathered for picnics, baseball in the yard, and dinners. Ours was a tight-knit family. We enjoyed our lives together. The MacKenzie family was a highly respected family in the community.

This was my world.

CHICKENS AND FIRECRACKERS

One of the supplements to the income of the farm was a small laying hen operation, where the eggs produced from a thousand laying hens were sold to neighbours and friends. The birds were housed in the west annex, in a second-storey room above the pig barn. The birds were housed on the floor with nests around the perimeter of the room. A small feed storage area was separated from the hens by a mesh fence from floor to ceiling. You got to this space by an outside staircase and then through an open doorway. It was my job to collect the eggs every day. I did not like this job one bit. If the birds were in their nests, they could sometimes peck at my hands. I hated the birds because they drew blood! When my grandfather gathered eggs, he would simply put his big hand under the bird, collect the eggs, saying, "I'm the boss." Every time he gathered eggs, he would open a cracked egg and swallow the raw egg whole. "It's the perfect food," he said. I agree.

One warm day in May, a school friend, Randy Wilson, came across the fields from the village to play. We were eleven years old—typical kids. Randy brought firecrackers. We took turns lighting them and throwing them into the air. Well, that activity soon became boring, so we began lighting the firecrackers and throwing them through the open upstairs door to the chicken house. You can imagine what happened. A big bang occurred followed by panicked squawking. Dust and feathers floated out of the door.

Randy and I took turns lighting and throwing the firecrackers. Noise, feathers, and dust were everywhere. It was great fun! We were engrossed in this game when my father came around the corner of the barn. He was coming to investigate what was causing all the commotion. When he discovered that Randy and I were the culprits, he shouted at Randy to "go home and don't come back!" Randy made a beeline over the fence and hightailed it across the fields toward his home. My father grabbed me by the scruff of the neck and took me up into the hayloft where he took a belt from the threshing machine and turned me over the pile of feedbags. I then received the spanking of a lifetime. I remember howling before the first blows landed.

After the spanking was over, my dad sat down beside me on the hay bales. He said that he gave the spanking for two reasons. The first one was that we were tormenting birds that provided an income. And it was no way to treat defenceless critters who probably wouldn't lay eggs for a week. The second reason was that he was very concerned about the fire hazard. Fire and dry farm buildings—with all the dust, straw, and other flammable materials—simply don't mix. He then told me that my grandfather had been through two barn fires in years past. These fires were caused by sparks from steam engines igniting chaff at grain harvesting time. Needless to say, they were very concerned about fire safety in and around the farm building.

Looking back on this incident, I realize that it took the spanking to cement the lessons that I needed to learn. I learned that the assets, in this case the buildings and hens used to generate income, need to be respected and maintained and not taken for granted and abused. I have also come to value the wisdom of my father's choice of educational method for this situation, even though I'm pretty sure I didn't sit down for two days.

LADDIE

Probably every farm has at least one dog. Many farms have more than one. Our farm was no exception.

Laddie was a male Border Collie dog. Border Collies are considered to be one of the most intelligent breeds of dogs. Laddie was very smart, exceedingly loyal, and displayed the typical colouring of the breed. He had been my dad's companion for ten years. He was a diligent but friendly watchdog, giving notice of every visitor. My father insisted that Laddie knew friends from strangers and that he signalled the difference by his bark. Laddie was always at my father's side. If Dad was working on the tractor doing fieldwork, Laddie ran alongside the tractor, loyally doing his duty. Occasionally his attention would be diverted when he caught the scent of a gopher or spied a crow that was trailing the cultivator. After the brief detours, he would resume his role as Dad's assistant.

Laddie, like all border collies, was a herding dog. My father would say "Laddie, get the cows," and off Laddie would dash, out to the fields to bring the cows back to the barn for milking. In his later years, Dad would insist that Laddie knew the cows by name and could cut a particular animal from the herd just by hearing the cow's name. I'm not sure this was true, but the story does illustrate the pride Dad took in his dog and the close relationship they had.

Laddie followed my father wherever he went on the farm. He was the quiet shadow in Dad's movement from chore to chore. All went well until I came along. One day, when I was about three years old, I was following Dad across the yard. As I was about to follow him into the chicken house when Laddie, with no warning, bit me on the side of my face. He was jealous of me. He had been the designated companion to my dad and apparently resented this strange new person taking his place. My mother rushed to take me to the doctor's office. The bite was perilously close to my eye. I nearly lost the sight of that eye. I remember the freezing and the stitches. When I got home, I noticed that Laddie was nowhere to be found. I was puzzled but thought little of it. It was a few years later that I learned that my father had taken a rifle and put Laddie down. When I talked to him in my adult years, he told me that, as much as he loved Laddie, he loved me more. He said that I was much, much more important to him than his intelligent, loyal companion, and that there was no hesitation whatsoever to do what he chose to do in putting Laddie down.

This lesson might have been lost on a three-year-old, but it certainly is not lost on me as an adult. Often, people wonder about their worth or value to their parents and their position or status in the family. Upon reflection, there is no question as to what my Dad thought of me. He was willing to sacrifice his beloved dog for me. My dad didn't say a lot. His action said much more than words. This story cemented my understanding of, and appreciation for, my father's love for me.

THE BIKE

Boys and bicycles belong together. Bikes represent one of the first passages to independence for a boy. First there is the tricycle, then a two-wheeler with training wheels. What a big day when those trainers came off! You felt as if you could travel anywhere, with no encumbrances or restraints. I was no exception to this pattern of mastering the skill of riding a bicycle.

The bike we had on the farm was, to put it mildly, a piece of junk. Its features were bald tires (white walls at that), one fender wired on to the frame, and a seat with no springs. The colour of the bike was a mottled, rusty grey. The chain never stayed on, and there were no grips on the handlebars. Nevertheless, we used, and used, and abused that bike.

Because the farm was very productive and situated on a well-travelled provincial highway, my dad and grandfather were often asked to hold demonstration days for farm equipment and provide test plots for seed companies wanting to display their latest hybrid seed. One year we were asked to use a ten-acre field bordering the highway as a demonstration site for a hybrid corn seed company. My grandfather agreed to do this. So, the varieties were sown and signs indicating the various strains were installed.

On a hot July day, my grandfather said to me, "Lad, do you want to earn yourself a new bike?"

I replied, "Sure would."

"Well," he said, "if you hoe that field of corn and satisfy my standards, you will have earned a new bike. Deal?"

Not fully knowing to what I was agreeing, I said "Deal." We shook hands on it. This was a really, really big deal to an eleven-year-old with a rusty bike.

The next Monday morning, I began the project. My grandfather gave me a freshly sharpened hoe, took me to the field, told me not to miss any weeds, and warned me to not hoe out any corn plants. Eagerly, I set to work. Starting at the edge row nearest to the barn, I flew at my work. Time seemed to fly by as I toiled in the heat and humidity typical of Ontario in July. All day long, I laboured. Up one row and down the next, I pulled big weeds and hoed out small ones, being careful not to miss a single weed. At the end of the day, I was surprised how little of the field I had covered. The reality of the size of the job began to dawn on me. But I had made a deal and I had to keep up my end of the bargain. And I wanted that bike!

Tuesday morning, I was back at the project. Row after row, hour after hour, I plugged away at the job. Evening's arrival was a welcome relief. Day after day, I was back at it. Occasionally, my grandfather would stop by and check my work, offer a word of encouragement, and then be on his way.

About three o'clock on Saturday, I finally finished my last row of corn. What a relief! I was exhausted but satisfied that I had made it through to the end of the job. I went and found my grandfather and said that I was ready for the field to be inspected. Together we walked to the field, my grandfather's hand resting lightly on my shoulder. He walked up and down a few rows, and then went to the far end of the field, where he did some more checking. I was very nervous. Would the job be good enough? Would he find deficiencies? Had I earned the bike?

Finally, my grandfather stood, turned to me and said, "Let's go get that bike." I was over the moon! I was so excited! I had thought that the bike would come someday, but we were going right now! Wow!

We drove into town and arrived at Balsdon's Hardware Store. My grandfather said to Mr. Balsdon, "This boy has earned a bike. Give him his pick." I looked over my choices. I did test rides. I checked out the brakes. I considered colour choices. Finally, I settled on my choice: a bright red bike with silver fenders. It was a simple bike with coaster breaks and red plastic handlebar grips. It was the most beautiful bike I had ever seen.

As we were heading to the cash register, my grandfather said to Mr. Balsdon, "This lad did a fantastic job. He has earned a basket and kick-stand as well. Please add those to the order." He was proud of me and satisfied with the job I had done!

As we left the store, he said, "I think you should ride it home." I could only nod my agreement. It was the ride of a lifetime. I was so pleased with my accomplishment and my choice of a bicycle. My parents met me as I rode up the lane to the farmyard. My mom cried and Dad gave me a small nod. I knew exactly what it meant. He was proud of me.

There were many lessons here: honour your deal; stick to the work; do your best; enjoy your rewards. It was the best bike ever!

SPRING

O n a farm, there is nothing like spring! As the sun begins to warm the earth, the snowbanks start to melt. Tiny rivulets of water run into the ditches; patches of green grass begin to emerge; migrating birds begin to return from the South; early spring flowers poke up from the cool earth; the hours of sunlight lengthen; the trees blossom. In short, the farm and all its residents awaken from their winter rest. I even noticed that my dad and granddad seemed to become more animated. As a boy, I didn't appreciate these rhythms. All I knew was that there would be lots more chores to do, some of which I dreaded and some of which I eagerly anticipated.

The most dreaded job in spring was "fixing fence." The livestock had been kept in barns over the harsh winter and now, as spring arrived, the cattle were soon to be let out to pasture. Befzre that could happen, however, we had to make sure that the fences were in good shape, ready to keep the livestock enclosed. Winter was hard on fences. Snowdrifts piled up in the fencerows, and the process of freezing and thawing would cause some of the strands of wire to sag, pull away from the posts, or even break. Our job was to walk the fence line and check every staple on every post, nailing wires up here, tightening barbwire there, splicing strands together as necessary. It was tedious, mind-numbing, far from glamorous work. I knew that it was a necessary ritual of spring, but that knowledge did nothing to ease how much I detested that job.

There were two things that did make the task more palatable. First of all, it was a job you performed with someone else, usually Grandpa. That made it more bearable. Even though there wasn't a lot of conversation, occasionally he would relate a story from his early days in Canada or talk about "The early spring of 1952." You learn about another person when you work beside them hour after hour. The second thing that made this job worthwhile was that after the fence was fixed, we could let the cows out to pasture for the season. They had been housed all winter in a confined space in the barn. Now, after three or four months, they were to be released to the outdoors. This was like getting out of school for summer vacation. Imagine seeing mature cows running, kicking up their heels like colts, cavorting in the lush new grass of spring. It was a sight to behold! After months of confinement, freedom was given. If dairy cows can experience so much joy after a few months in a warm barn with lots of bedding and good feed, I wonder what it was like for Nelson Mandela to experience freedom after twenty-four years in a small cell with no view, and only a bedroll and a chair. Seeing the cows enjoy springtime freedom made fixing fence worth it. But I still didn't like it!

In contrast to the drudgery of fixing fence, getting ready to get our yearly shipment of baby chicks was exciting. Dairy farming was the main business of the farm, but we also grew meat chickens every year. There was a brooder house on the farm. It was an insulated building about the size of a double garage. It was equipped with hanging feeders, water drinkers, and adjustable overhead heaters. We would turn the heat on about a week before the chicks arrived. Then we went to the sawmill and bought a load of shavings. There was a distinctly pleasant aroma as we spread the shavings over the floor of the brooder house. Then we rolled out a ring of corrugated cardboard in a circle under the heaters and around the feeders and drinkers. The room was ready for the arrival of the bundles of fluff to be delivered.

There is a special symbolism to baby chicks. These yellow bundles of fluff, each weighing a couple of ounces, only a day old, were carefully placed in the warm fragrant shavings. I remember the way my grandfather carefully handled these delicate chicks with his strong but gentle hands, hands that could easily crush the baby birds. The balance of strength and gentleness is not innate but learned. The way Grandpa handled these birds is a constant reminder to me about the need to find that balance in my words and deeds. Fluffy baby chicks continue to draw me back to the new beginnings of spring.

Spring also meant that we were soon to be on the land preparing the soil for planting. Plowing, tilling, cultivating the land represented the initiation of a new season, a new cycle, the prospect of income that comes from the careful stewardship of the land. As a boy, it was interesting to watch the stages and activities that unfolded as spring emerged. It started with getting the farm machinery out of their winter storage, checking belts and chains, and oiling and greasing all the necessary areas of the equipment so that everything was in working order once the truly busy planting season began. It seemed like events occurred in a haphazard way, but as the seasons unfolded year after year, I saw the intentionality of preparing and tilling the soil, planting the seeds, and scheduling the timing of activities. There was a fluidity about the timing of these events and actions. A farmer uses the calendar but also must 'listen' to the weather and the warming of the soil. If you worked the ground too soon, the soil could become compacted and unreceptive to planting and impede the germination and growth of the seeds. However, if you waited too long, the growing season was too short, and the crop didn't yield as much as expected.

I watched and helped in these seasonal activities. One time, when I was a young teen, I thought I knew it all. The spring had been warm and dry, and several of the neighbouring farmers were working the land. I pushed and pestered Dad and Grandpa, insisting we were lagging behind. Finally, my dad said, "Okay. If you think you know everything, go ahead. Take the tractor and disc and get started on the fieldwork." I headed out to the field, eager to get going. I hitched up the tractor and disc and started out along the fence row. After about one hundred metres, the disc filled with mud; the tractor bogged down and I was nearly stuck. I managed to extract the disc and tractor, returning to the farmyard. My grandfather met me in the yard. He said, "Lad, our farm is not like the neighbour's farm. Our soil is different. Our goals are different. Our soil looked dry, but because we used manure as fertilizer, there is more moisture under the surface. That's why you got stuck. Our time will come, and our results will be better for our farm if we are patient." He said he was glad I had that experience, saying that he was certain that it would be a good base for life decisions in my future.

Experience is a good teacher, but only if we learn from it. Experience simply for experience's sake is useless unless we apply the lessons. If I had gone back on the wet fields the next year, the first year's events would have been useless. I would have been increasingly frustrated if I hadn't applied what I learned that early spring day. This lesson has been taught in many ways, many times, over my childhood. Building on the experiences of life equips me to handle more and more challenges and opportunities coming my way.

Each crop requires its own preparation, and each crop has its time to be sown. For example, if corn seed was sown too early in the year, the seed would rot in the wet ground or the seedlings could die from a late frost, thus ruining the yields and potential profit. In a similar way, barley or oats need to be seeded earlier in the spring. First, they can handle the wetter soil and cooler conditions. Moreover, if they are seeded too late, then the hot summer days will stunt the growth and yields. Every crop has its criteria for a successful outcome. Agricultural science and the 'art' of crop husbandry meld to produce the optimum yield.

There is a good lesson here, too. Doing what is necessary and timely yields the best outcome. Acting rashly and impulsively, and in an untimely manner, often leads to unfortunate outcomes. At the same time, listening to our intuition or inner ear supports the application of knowledge and experience.

It is so satisfying to till the soil and sow the seeds. A few days after seeding, my grandpa and I would walk the fields. Periodically, we would crouch down and scratch under the surface, looking for the sown seeds. We were looking for signs of germination. We were relieved and exhilarated when we found that the seeds were sprouting. We were on the right track. This activity was necessary because, if there was no germination, it meant that the seed was bad, and we had to adjust our plans. If there was time, we could reseed the same crop. But if it was too late, we would have to change to a different crop, revising the crop plan for the year. This process of early monitoring was essential to avoid bad surprises later. What a good lesson for life! Continuous monitoring, re-evaluation, and necessary adjustments help me avoid experiences that could change the course of my life journey.

A few days later, you could see a soft green tint over the fields. The seeds were sprouting! Growth was happening! Now we could begin the care of these crops. Irrigation, fertilization, and weed control were all part of working with nature to see a bountiful crop. This was not a 'one size fits all' process. Different crops, different fields, and different weather indicated the required husbandry on our part. Again, observation, science, and experience all worked in harmony to try to have the best outcome. I am still amazed at the ease with which Dad and Grandpa melded all the factors needed for a good crop. More importantly, there was an underlying trust that they had done all they could do, and that having done so, they could now rest and allow natural processes to unfold. Grandpa often said, "We can't control the rain."

Why worry about things you can't control? If you have done your best in a timely manner, relax and look forward to the outcome with eagerness. Imagine the time we would save and the stress we would avoid if we took worry from our lives.

SUMMER

Even though our calendars designate a specific date for the change of seasons, nature moves seamlessly throughout the year. On a farm, particularly a dairy farm, there is no "off" season. In spring, when all the tilling and planting was happening, there was no end to the daily chores and activities on our farm. The cows had to be milked twice a day, every day. The eggs had to be collected every day. The cropping activities had to be layered on the daily chores. And the attention to these chores couldn't be allowed to slip. Planting the big garden was also an important job that got worked in as time allowed.

I was very aware that there was no grumbling about the increased busyness, but that it was accepted simply as part of the rhythm of farm life.

If spring was busy, the summer was even busier. We had no more than finished planting the grain crops when it was time to begin the process of harvesting. The first crop needing to be harvested was the forage crop. Grass and forage crops grow rapidly in spring. Harvesting the forage crop in a timely manner was very important. We wanted to maximize the nutrient content of the hay crop. Hay and corn silage form the main portion of a dairy cow's diet, and so, if you want to get a lot of milk, you have to have a really high-quality silage and hay. Again, there is an art, an intuition, about when to cut the grass and alfalfa crop. Once cut, you needed to bale the hay at precisely the right time. The baled hay would mold if it was baled too wet and would lose nutrients if it was baled too dry. Hay formed a major part of the diet of our dairy herd. We baled about fifteen thousand bales of hay every year. These bales weighed sixty pounds each. After cutting, the hay was raked into rows and allowed to dry. At the right moisture, we then began to bale the hay. Dad drove the baler, and it fell to me or my brother to ride a sled attached to the baler. As the bales were formed, they slid from the baler to the sled. I would grab the bale and stack it in a wedge-shaped pyramid, six bales to each wedge. Then it was dropped to the ground to dry until we came to get it later. Baling started about noon, when the moisture level of the hay was correct, and continued until dusk, when the dew started to descend. It was long, hot work, but it made a young man strong! The bales were handled three times. First the baling, then loading the wagons, and finally storing in the haylofts. Remember that none of the other chores could be neglected while the baling went on. The whole family pitched in. Grandma was responsible for the field lunches. Several times throughout the day and into the evening, she would bring sandwiches and tea to the field and replenish the water jugs. We would sit in the shade while we enjoyed these feasts. And feasts they were to a hot, hungry teen. Then we went back to work, trying to finish the day's work before dark. If we were done early enough, we took a short ride in the old international pickup truck to Whiteman's Creek for a swim in the cool water. This was the best way to get the hay chaff washed off our hot bodies. Grandpa would say, "Work first, then play." He was right. Play is far more enjoyable when the work is done.

Once the hay crop was in the barn, the grain crops of wheat, barley, and oats were ready for harvesting. In my late teen years, we had a combine for this harvest. Before the arrival of the combine, we threshed our grain crops. This entailed cutting the grain with a binder, which made bundles of grain and then dropped them on the ground. Then, we followed the binder, gathered up the sheaves of grain, and 'stooked' several of these bundles or sheaves in a stack that was designed to shed the rain until the threshing machine arrived at the farm. My dad and his two brothers, who had their own farms, shared the use of the machine, as well as the work they we had to do.

These threshing events were big deals. At noon, we washed under the apple tree and then had a big meal of roast beef, fresh tomatoes, corn on the cob, and three or four pies all prepared by Grandma and my mother. Then we had a fifteen-minute nap before we went back to work. It was both exciting and a relief to see the grain finally in the bin and the straw in the mow. The careful planning and work done in spring were finally rewarded.

The important lesson for me was that choices have consequences. We could have chosen to not plant the grain, but the consequence would be no crop. That is an extreme example, but in a less dramatic way, I will reap the consequences later in life from bad health or lifestyle choices in my younger years. This law of the farm, of reaping what you sow, pervades every aspect of life, whether it is health and diet, financial management, or relationships. We can't get away from it. I appreciate learning this lesson in such a tangible way early in my life.

AUTUMN

Autumn follows summer as surely as night follows day. Days begin to shorten, but often the weather is delightful, with warm sunny days and crisp, cool evenings. The trees begin to change colour. The garden produce needs to be harvested. Apples need to be picked. Potatoes need to be dug. This time of year continues to be very busy. The ongoing daily chores continue and require the consistent diligence that successfully produces milk. Along with the regular activities, there were a couple of big events that marked autumn.

The corn crop we planted in May was now ready for harvesting. Corn silage is a major component of a cow's diet. Harvesting at the right stage of maturity dictated the quality and quantity of nutrients in the silage. We did not own the expensive harvesting equipment but contracted the work to people who specialized in this kind of harvesting. It was so exciting for me as a young boy to see the big machinery drive up the lane. There was going to be action for a couple of days!

Silo filling, as we called it, was a time for action. "All hands on deck," was the word of the day. Getting the crop into the silo as quickly as possible was absolutely necessary. My job, as a teenager, was to be in the silo as the chopped-up corn stalks and cobs were blown up into the circular tower. As the crop was blown into the silo, we had to tramp around and around the silo to ensure that the silage was packed down tightly to ensure there were no air pockets. It was hard work to stay ahead of the silage pouring in. It was also dangerous because you could easily get swamped. It seemed as if there was a death from silo filling every year in the county. Dad and Grandpa were very concerned that every job on the farm was done safely, and this was no exception. The reward for this work was a high-quality crop that the animals ate eagerly, and they rewarded the good diet with a full pail of milk.

The second big event in autumn was doing preparatory fieldwork before winter set in. The crops had been harvested, and now the fields were mostly bare. The corn field had stalks and stubble. This residue was an important part of our crop production practice. We needed to turn the crop residue under the ground so it could decompose and provide nutrients for the next year's crop cycle.

I loved this process of plowing. The act of turning something unsightly into something useful was satisfying.

Plowing straight furrows brought me pressure. In rural communities there were annual county and provincial "plowing matches." These matches were competitions between farmers to see who could produce the best plowing result. Ploughmen were judged on the uniformity of the plowing, how completely the sod was turned over, and other intangibles. The pressure on me came from the fact that both my granddad and father were champion ploughmen. Grandpa MacKenzie was provincial champion using a two-horse team to pull the plow. Dad was a champion for "all-round best ploughman" in the county. So, when I got the task of plowing, it came with specific instructions. There were instructions about how deep to plow, how fast to drive, which way to turn at the end of the field, and on and on. These instructions seemed senseless to me. After all, turning the sod appeared simple. I soon learned that these directives had a purpose. The process of decomposition was enhanced if the sod was fully turned under. The spring soil preparation went better if the job was done well. The most important instruction was plowing straight and true furrows. Grandpa and Dad said that doing this job indicated how seriously we took our responsibility as stewards of the land. A straight furrow was a visible display of care and attention. Over and over, I heard the words, "A job worth doing is a job worth doing well." How true. The approach to any task, project or initiative must be defined by me giving it my best effort. A job well done gets noticed. Dad always said, "'Just okay' is not okay." Plowing taught me that lesson!

WINTER

With harvesting all done and the fall field work finished, the routines on the farm settled into the winter rhythms. Cows were not feeding on pasture but housed in the dairy barn. There were still many daily chores that had to continue. Feeding, milking, cleaning, and other daily chores continued. Winter brought new chores and challenges. We lived in an area where there were regular and deep snowfalls. So, one ongoing job was snow removal. The milk truck came every two days to pick up the milk and deliver it to the processing plant. We had to keep the lanes and yard clear of snow so the truck could get to the farm. I remember one year when we had to clear snow for twenty-three days straight. This is just one example of the new jobs that filled the days on the farm in winter.

However, winter allowed our farm to become calmer and more settled, with less pressure and urgency. There was more time to groom the cattle, perform repair jobs, and think about new ways to do things around the farm.

The dairy barn was a warm space. The cattle's body heat made the building very comfortable to work in. The smells of the silage, the fresh hay, and the animal odours were pleasant. Memories flood back to me when I catch a whiff of those distinctive farm smells today.

In the other seasons we focused on the crops, but in winter we had the time to pay particular attention to the animals. I loved working with the cows and calves. They responded to my attention. The cows needed their hooves trimmed, their coats brushed, and their tails combed. They liked it a lot! It was fun to add fresh straw to the bedding under the cows and the see them settle into the bedding to chew their cud. You could almost hear them sigh with contentment. It was interesting to observe the rhythm of the cows. After being milked they ate their feed, then settled down in their straw bedding and began chewing their cud. I remember asking Granddad what was going on when a cow chewed its cud. He replied, "A cow chews its cud for a couple of reasons. First, chewing the cud is the cow's way of digesting its food and preparing itself for producing more milk. But," he said, "look at the contentment on a cow's face as it chews its cud. It's as if the animal is saying, 'My life is good.'" Grandpa chewed his "cud," so to speak, when he sat on the porch and smoked his pipe every evening. He used this time to relax, reflect on his day, and begin to settle down for the night. In our busy, frantic world, we need to learn to "chew our cud."

My granddad said that winter was our opportunity to pamper our animals. "We are their caregivers," he said. "We rely on them for our income, and we must be good to them." This principle of stewardship is critical in all aspects of our lives. I need to be a good steward of the resources I have. I need to take care of my relationships. I need to tend to my health. If I abuse any of these areas in my life, I lose in so many ways—income, relationships, contentment—just as we would lose income if we didn't take proper care of our cows.

My father and grandfather used winter to do some things that were critical for success in the other seasons. One activity was to sit down and plan what crops were to be planted in which field, and how many tons of grain or how many acres of silage were needed. Which fields would be planted with which crops? It was necessary to do both short-term and long-term planning, which were both critical for a successful farm operation. Effective and intentional planning is key to our lives. It was good to see how my elders planned and then observe the results of that planning. This feedback loop is an important way we learn and adjust to our world.

The other main winter job was to do any necessary major repairs on the farm machinery. You wanted to have the equipment to be ready to go when spring came. Waiting to do repairs on the machinery until you needed it in the spring could cost you time and productivity. Doing what is important when it is not urgent always results in more success. There are enough surprises in any endeavour without adding in the unnecessary pressure of a deadline.

Winter was an important season on the farm. I believe that outcomes and results would have been disappointing the rest of the year if we didn't have winter. Winter is a time for preparation, reflection, recuperation, repairing, and re-energization. Our world needs to welcome the winters in our lives. We will be better for it.

ANIMALS

On any livestock farm, the animals are the focus. The animals generate the income. The animals literally are the partners of the farmer. If the animals are not well cared for, the farm won't be a success. My father and grandfather emphasized, again and again, that a farmer had to be a good steward of the resources on the farm, whether it was the land or the livestock. Careful attention to the health, nutrition, and well-being of the cows was always the first priority on the farm. After that, other priorities fell into place. Setting the correct priorities is critical to a life that is fulfilling and complete. I need to be a good steward of the resources I have been given, whether it is my intelligence, health, finances, or other skills and gifts.

The idea of stewardship, and what good stewardship looks like, was easy to see on our farm. My dad would regularly walk among the cattle, looking for any symptoms of poor health. He would check for infections, swelling of joints, limps, sore feet, and other visible signs of ill health. If an animal was discovered to be ailing, she was separated into a 'sick' pen where any necessary individual attention was required. If the issue was discovered soon enough, we could put the animal back on the road to recovery ourselves. Occasionally, however, we had to call the veterinarian. It was serious if my dad or grandpa said, "We'd better call the Doc."

Doc Beatty was the area vet, specializing in large animal medicine. As a young boy, I was awestruck by this man's the ability to diagnose the issue with the animal quickly and easily, give a necessary injection, or leave medication for us to administer after he had left. His bedside manner was gentle yet assertive, with the cow trusting this stranger to tend to her sickness or injury.

Becoming a vet was one of my early goals. In fact, I was accepted into veterinary school at The University of Guelph, Ontario. The school was elite in North America. Over six hundred applications were received for a class of forty students. My family was very proud of the fact that I had been accepted into this program. I was the first MacKenzie in our extended family of fifteen cousins to attend university, let alone getting into vet school. After my acceptance, I began to wonder what I was in for. I asked our veterinarian about the implications of attending vet school and what my work career would be like. He said, "Son, whatever career you choose, you need to love it. You need to be able to say that there was nothing else that you could think of that you would rather do."

His words caused me to begin to rethink my decision to accept the placement at the vet college. I simply could not envision my future as a veterinarian. So, much to the surprise of many people, I turned down the invitation to go to vet school. It is interesting to see how the choices we make affect our life, either in the near or distant future. I did not understand it at the time, but I know now that I rejected this opportunity because somehow, in my inner being, I knew that this life path was not for me, and that my life journey was to take a different route. I continued my studies, getting my honours degree in Agricultural Science, and went on to obtain a master's degree in animal nutrition. These degrees led to a fulfilling career in agriculture, allowing me to stay closely connected to my farm roots. The decision I made in my youth provided me with a very satisfying career in livestock feed manufacturing—a career that allowed me to travel the world, impact agricultural policy, and provide a very comfortable lifestyle. Dr. Beatty's advice was right! Doing what I loved enriched my life. At the same time, I still marvel at the skills of the veterinarian community as they tend to animals' health needs.

A good steward of the animals is required to plan ways to improve the animals' productivity. This planning and learning were ever-present on the farm. The cows' milk production was carefully monitored. Questions like, "Does she need more grain?" or, "Should we adjust the protein level of the feed?" were constantly being asked. My dad was also always trying to improve the overall quality of the animals. This was done by carefully matching the cow's traits with an appropriate semen donor. What bull would sire a calf that would produce more than her mother? Dad studied journals and industry reports, listened to recommendations from the vet, and carefully evaluated the theoretical results if a particular sire was used. These decisions were not taken lightly. And the results of those decisions were not known for at least two years. Dad kept careful records of his decisions and would evaluate their results as the years went by. This decision cycle was a very effective way to improve the quality of the herd. The choices Dad made about the cows had consequences, literally measured by the productivity of the herd.

In life, choices have consequences. My choice to not attend vet school had life-changing consequences for me. Some choices are not as critical as others, but all choices have consequences. Could I have received a better grade on a course if I had studied instead of going to the movies? Would I have made the sale if I had been better prepared? Questions and decisions like these, whether intentional or not, influence the journey of our lives in small and large ways. I learned this life lesson as I watched and listened to the ways dad and Granddad made choices—some intuitive, some intentional, some by accident, but all of them consequential. The phrase, "Choices have consequences" is an absolute truth.

FAIRS

When I was growing up, nearly every community held an annual event, the Fall Fair, which was one of the key social and cultural events of rural Ontario. The Fall Fair is hard to describe. It is a blend of carnival, competition, exhibition, and social activities. Our village, Burford, like most other communities, had its annual Fall Fair. It was held annually for three days over the Thanksgiving weekend.

The Fair grounds was a large acreage on the edge of town. It had a half-mile horse racetrack, exhibit halls, a grandstand, cattle, and horse and sheep sheds. A typical weekend at Burford Fair included harness horse races, horseshoe competitions, a baby beauty pageant (which my younger brother won one year), cooking demonstrations, arts and crafts displays, a carnival with a Ferris wheel, and more. It was a big event. Everyone attended and most participated in some way. Dad was very involved in the Burford Fair, acting as president for several years. My mother was named Queen of the Fair one year.

My grandmother displayed her pies and baked goods, often getting many first-place ribbons. My grandfather was a judge of the horse show, where horses and wagons were compared for uniformity, fit, finish, and handling.

I was very involved in the dairy cattle competition. Animals were paraded around the show ring and compared to other animals of the same age and breed. There is an art to "showing" cattle. There was a lot involved in preparing the animal to be shown. Washing, brushing, combing, hoof trimming, and, most importantly, handling were all critical to winning the coveted first-place ribbons. I learned to handle the cattle from my grandfather. He had a knack for training the cow to walk properly and stand correctly so he could show the judge the cow's best attributes. It was a lot of work. Training had to start weeks and weeks before show day. The showmen wore a pure white shit and pair of pants so the focus was on the animal, not its showman.

I learned well. I was able to show a mediocre animal so well that the judge often liked my animal more than a better one. Over time, my skill was noticed, and I began to be invited to show animals for other cattle owners at other fairs in other towns. As a teenager in a rural area, this local fame was pretty cool. Soon, I was on the fair circuit, making good cash from this skill, learned from Grandpa MacKenzie.

The biggest fair was in Toronto. The Royal Agricultural Winter Fair was the Super Bowl of fall fairs and lasted two weeks, with many different competitions and events. I showed cattle many times at this huge fair. One of the events was a showmanship competition. The judge evaluated your ability to show the animal to its best advantage. Did the animal stand correctly? Was the showman too obvious, or was the animal the star? This event is a farm boy's all-star game. As it turned out, I edged out my cousin, Keith, for the grand prize ribbon—and a nice cheque, too.

The big event every night was the horse show jumping competition. A crowd of eight thousand people filled the arena to see the competition. Part of the way through the horse event, the prize winners of that day's cattle show were paraded for the crowd to acknowledge. As a good showman, I was often privileged to participate in this event. This was pretty heady stuff for a small-town boy. My grandfather kept me grounded. He said, "If your head gets too big, you will lose. You and the animal are a team. You are nothing without a good partner." His words echo in my ears today. "Let other people praise you. Never do it yourself."

As I reflect on my Fall Fair experiences, I appreciate the sense of community that the fairs engendered. I appreciate the opportunity I had to compete in the various showman competitions, learning what it is like to be on stage, so to speak. Most importantly, learning to handle wins and losses with grace and humility are the really important prize ribbons in my life.

4-H CLUB

When I was growing up, 4-H Club was an activity for rural teenagers involved in agriculture. 4-H stands for Head, Heart, Hands, and Health. The purpose of 4-H Club was to provide a social and educational venue for farm kids, teaching the benefits of a balanced life. There were clubs dedicated to different aspects of agriculture. For example, you could be a member of the crop club, the swine club, or the horticulture club. I was a member of the dairy club and the crop club. Monthly meetings were held at the farms of the club members, rotating from farm to farm. There was an educational portion, where we would learn some aspect of dairy farming or crop husbandry. There were also tours of manufacturing plants devoted to agricultural production. For example, we toured the Kellogg's Corn Flakes plant in our area to learn how the grain grown on our farms was transformed into cereal for human consumption.

The most important part of any club was the annual project. In the diary club, we had to choose a calf from our herd. Over the eight months of the club season, we were responsible to monitor growth, feeding regimens, and so on. At the end of the season, we took our calf to the local Fall Fair to show them in the dairy cattle show. The competition was keen. All the animals were primped and prepared for the show. We were marked on our presentation, our reports, and the show competition. I had strong support from Dad and Granddad. They were eager to have me visit other dairy farms and see how other farmers ran their farms.

4-H Clubs taught me a lot! Sometimes I would pick up a tip how on to do a chore or job that we weren't doing so well on our farm. Often, I learned that the things we were doing on our farm were being done pretty well. It gets easy to think that everyone else is better at what they do than yourself. Seeing how others do things is instructive and useful. I learned that there is much to be gained from an objective assessment of myself, my ability, my skills, and my performance. In my career, I took every opportunity to visit other businesses in my industry to compare notes with other business leaders and look at industry innovations. Just as in 4-H club, sometimes I learned something new and innovative—something that we could apply to our business. More often, though, I learned that the things we were doing were the best way for us. 4-H club was a key part of my understanding this principle: for success, I must continually evaluate, assess, and re-evaluate the processes in my business. This principle is critical to improving outcomes in my business and life.

Another major part of 4-H dairy club was the judging competition. In the judging competition, there was a group of four animals shown to the club members. Our task was to judge the cattle and their traits and rank them in order from one to four. You could make notes justifying your choices and your ranking. There are specific physical traits in an animal that are indicators of productivity. Our task was to evaluate these animals against the breed standards and against the other animals in the class. The difficult part was that you were expected, when asked, to give a short summary of the reasons behind your ranking. You did not have a chance to prepare. You had to speak when asked. Your reasoning for your order of best to worst went something like this: "Mister Chairman, fellow judges, I placed this class of three-year-old Guernsey milking cows 2,4,1,3. I placed cow number 2 over number 4 because…" and I would give a few reasons. Similarly, I would have to go through all the cows, comparing them and giving reasons for my placement. Then I would say, "Mister Chairman, for these reasons, I placed this class 2,4,1,3."

Every judge would give his or her reasons. Then, the instructor gave his reasons for his placings. It was nerve-wracking but potentially rewarding to hear how you did in these judging classes. Points were awarded for the season. Winners were invited to a season-ending competition at the Royal Agricultural Winter Fair, where you judged against other 4-H Club members from across Ontario. I competed in this final event three times, with a second-place ribbon on two occasions.

Learning to speak, off the cuff, without notes, in a clear concise manner, whether it is in front of just a few people or a crowd of several hundred, is a skill that has proved exceedingly useful in my work and life. 4-H Club is the reason that I can be comfortable when presented with the need or opportunity to speak in public.

DOCTORS, HEALTH, HEALING

As I think about my childhood and youth, I see how many events in our farm family have influenced my attitude and approach to my own health. In our rural community, we had a great local doctor. Doc McIntyre was a fixture in Burford, highly respected and skilled at taking good care of his patients. My first remembrance of Doc McIntyre was the day that I was given stitches near my eye after I was bitten by Laddie, my father's loyal dog. I remember that Doc McIntyre was gentle, efficient, and kind. I had the sense that he was a person that you went to for repairs or adjustments. Just as a mechanic fixes a flat tire, I believed that doctors were there to fix a broken body if we determined that it was too serious for it to be fixed by ourselves.

When it wasn't serious, we turned to the herbal, folksy remedies as the means to recover. Mustard plasters were the designated solution for chest congestion. Raleigh's Salve was "prescribed" for general aches and pains. No need for Advil or Aspirin as long as you had Raleigh's on the shelf. Cuts, scrapes, and bruises were treated with a reddish "paint" called Mercurochrome. This stinging paint was used generously on young boys who invariably had lots of cuts and wounds. We were also regularly subjected to a dose of castor oil. It was widely believed that castor oil was the preventative for colds and flu. Maybe it worked, but it tasted awful.

The favourite home cure was Absorbine. This was literally a liniment for horses. If your horse had muscular or joint soreness, swelling, or stiffness, this foul-smelling liquid was used. It was only a small leap to use Absorbine on a human body. After a hard day's work, we would often slather it on our aching muscles and sore joints. After the liniment was applied, you would feel your body heat up. And it seemed to work. My grandfather, who worked hard every day of his life, had an Absorbine aroma blended with his pipe tobacco. Whenever we would say, "Grandpa, take it easy and take a rest," he would respond by reminding us that the liniment bottle said, "After application, work the horse."

As an adult, I am not judging the use of these home remedies. Our family was healthy. And we did not have many prescriptions in the medicine cabinet. In fact, my dad would say, "I'd rather pay the grocer than the pharmacist." He meant that healthy food was preferable to a pharmaceutical product. Over the years, the pendulum has swung away from these kinds of home remedies to overeager use of manufactured pharmaceuticals. Thankfully, there is a renewed interest in, and evaluation of, some of these ancient medicinal herbs and salves. These home remedies were a significant part of my childhood, but they unfortunately gave me a cynical and negative attitude to pharmaceuticals, many of which have saved many lives. There is a need for a balanced approach to the wise use of pharmaceuticals coupled with the well-known benefits of natural supplements and ointments.

My grandfather was a strong, hard-working man, even into his older years. This strength often got him into difficulty. I remember one example of how tough he was and how he used Doc McIntyre's services.

One day, Grandpa was carrying two hundred-pound sacks of grain on his shoulders across the barn floor. As he stepped over a door sill, he tripped and pitched forward. With all that weight on his shoulders, he wasn't able to break his fall. As he fell forward, his chin hit the narrow edge of a wooden frame. His jaw was jammed up, with his bottom teeth locked together with his top teeth. His jaw broken and his teeth jammed, we took him to the doctor.

Doc McIntyre examined Grandpa and said, "I need to talk to the dentist." After the dentist arrived and took a look at Grandpa, he and the doctor went into the next room to discuss what to do. A few minutes later, we heard my grandfather say, "I got it, Doc."

When the doctor and dentist came into the examination room, they discovered that Grandpa had grabbed the top and bottom rows of his teeth in each hand and pulled his jaws apart. Problem solved! Doc McIntyre wired up the jaws. The dentist pulled the broken teeth. Grandpa went home.

Like most families in the time health issues were common. In the forties, polio was a feared infectious disease. This disease attacked young people seemingly at random, causing many deaths and even more physical disabilities. For no apparent reason, my father contracted polio when he was twenty-eight years old. This was about a decade older than the average age of contracting the disease.

The standard treatment was to put the patient in isolation in a special ward in the hospital. Dad was hospitalized for several months. Upon his release, he spent about two years undergoing extensive physical therapy. The result of the disease was that my father's whole left side was partially paralyzed. The muscles down his left side were atrophied, leaving him with an arm and leg that were weak. He walked with a significant limp. His left arm was spindly, with the only joint that worked being his thumb.

This is the only way that I knew my dad. I never considered him to be disabled. He farmed his whole life with these limitations. His body adapted to the deficiencies it had. Dad's right arm and leg did all the work. He handled bales of hay one-handed. He milked cows, did field work, and largely set the pace of work for everyone. I never, ever, heard him complain!

My mother and father were engaged to be married when Dad contracted polio. Dad wanted Mom to move on and find a new man. She replied with an emphatic, "No! No disease or adversity will stop me from being your wife. You are the one for me!"

Mom visited Dad every day while he was in isolation and helped him do his rehabilitation exercises at home. Her unwavering commitment and devotion to my dad shine as a bright light of remembrance in my mind.

My father's experience with polio taught me valuable lessons about how to deal with adversity. I was in sixth grade when I was injured in an accident at recess at school. A bunch of us kids were kicking a soccer ball around the school yard. I was pushed by another kid and fell hard on a pile of cinders. A big shard of cinder penetrated my right knee. The school nurse pulled the cinder from my knee, put a bandage on it, and sent me back to class. A few days later, my knee swelled up to twice its size, to the point where I couldn't bend it. I went to the doctor, where a swab was taken. The next day I was admitted to the hospital and put in an isolation ward, where I was treated with antibiotics and hot compresses designed to reduce the swelling. I was in the hospital for a week with this infection. I was allowed to go home after they determined that the infection was gone. Seemingly, life was back to normal.

In grade seven, at age thirteen, I began feeling pain in my right knee. I limped. My parents thought I was making this pain up and looking for attention. They would watch me when I wasn't looking to see if I limped only when they were looking. One day, I was in the local general store with my dad. As we left the store, my dad was frustrated that I wasn't coming along with him. But I couldn't move my right leg. It wouldn't work. The knee and hip were locked up.

The next day, I was at the doctor's office. He sent me to an orthopaedic surgeon who diagnosed my issue as Legg Perthes disease. This disease is a bacterial degenerative disease of the hip. It occurs more frequently in young boys than girls, and it is usually treated by putting the legs in a cast for three months so that the hip bones can regenerate. In my case, the fall on the cinder pile was judged to be the cause of my Legg Perthes. Because I was a young teen, which made me old for this disease, the method of treatment was to design a brace for my leg that completely removed any weight from the damaged leg. This brace had a hinge at the knee, so I was able to bend the leg, but my foot couldn't touch the ground because my leg was strapped into a metal frame where my weight was carried on my pelvis. The intent was to allow the diseased hip to completely rebuild itself. To allow for the leg to stay off the ground, the sole of my left shoe was built up two inches. I wore this apparatus for nearly three years.

As a kid, initially I thought that I was a kind of celebrity. This wore off very quickly. I had been an active boy, running, skating, playing baseball—simply doing all the things a young teen does. Overnight, I was sidelined.

A child's early teens are important formative years, and they go a long way to defining who a boy will become as an adult. It was a difficult time for me. I was athletic and involved in a lot of sports. I was active on the farm. Life was great! Suddenly, I felt like I didn't belong. I was an outsider. I began to feel sorry for myself. I don't remember how long this self-pity lasted, but I do know that my dad was the one who pulled me out of this low point. He told me, "Your life isn't over. You will recover and be fully normal. The more you obey the instructions from the doctors, the faster you will be out of the brace. And," he added, "this doesn't mean you get out of doing your chores. You can still walk and lift and think. Let's get to work."

This was a wake-up call for me. My father was a victim of polio. He persevered and overcame his disability living a full, hard-working life all without complaint. Who was I to "cry in my cornflakes," as my grandfather would say? This pep talk and the daily example of my father were strong visual and verbal lessons for me. I didn't want to let Dad down. I wanted to be like him. So, I did my chores, looked for diversions to replace the loss of sports, and listened to the doctors. It was a great day when I took that brace off for the last time! My dad was right!

Subsequently, I played competitive baseball, high school basketball, and university soccer. My regenerated hip worked! The doctors indicated that as a midlife adult, I would likely experience arthritis in my hip. This was true. I stayed very active through my adult years, but bit by bit, the hip wore out to the point where it couldn't do its job. At age forty-eight, I received a replacement for my right hip. Through this surgical miracle, I am free of pain and leading an active, normal life.

I am grateful for the example of my father, the way he dealt with the effects of polio, and how he taught me in word and deed to not wallow in self-pity, but to literally embrace situations and overcome any adversity. I'm also grateful for my grandfather who often "played hurt," carrying on with his life and work with a smile and determination, even with the aches, pains, and injuries. I'm grateful that I have been able to find the balance between ignoring the medical world and running to the doctor for every little thing. And I'm grateful for the medical advances and discoveries that allow me to enjoy the life that I have. I'm even grateful for the Absorbine liniment and Raleigh's Salve.

VACIATIONS

On most farms, but especially on small family dairy farms, there are no days off. It seemed as if a vacation was a Sunday afternoon nap. Day after day, the chores were unending. Jobs and tasks came at us in an unrelenting stream. Growing up on our farm, I never realized that most people expected a vacation or holiday. The annual two-week stay at the cottage or trip to Florida was unheard of, let alone expected. As a kid, I never missed such trips.

As an adult, I ask myself, "Why didn't I miss a vacation?" When I think about my life as a young person on our farm, I realize that there were many, many "vacations." Clearly, these vacations are not the kind of holiday considered "normal" by most people. But I see now that there were interludes in the rhythm of our life that eased the drudgery and boredom of the daily routine. These interludes were both intentional and unintentional.

I guess a better word for "vacation" on our farm is the word "play." We played a lot! What am I talking about? Well, I'm talking about things like a full-contact game of road hockey that would often break out when my cousins came over to our place and we walked back to the house after evening milking. Or the game of darts in the back kitchen after the noon meal. The darts were always ready for action. Dad would say, "You ready?" I would nod, and the game was on. We would play a quick game of 501. Then Dad would nod and say, "Okay, let's get back to work." This kind of mini "vacation" happened all the time.

My favourite "vacation" was playing soccer on the lawn after chores were done on a warm summer evening. We had makeshift goal posts set up, and the ball was always sitting there, ready for action. If some cousins showed up, we would have a real game, but most often, we took turns being the goaltender, and one brother took shots on goal. We gained a lot of skill playing soccer in the yard. I became good enough that I was able to play varsity soccer with the University of Guelph. So, the soccer "vacation turned out well for me.

There was always a ball or a stick around. We would pick up the baseball gloves and toss the ball around. Or we would take turns being pitcher and catcher, pretending we were in the big leagues. Again, the backyard baseball games turned into me being a starting infielder on an amateur fast pitch baseball team that went to the provincial play-offs.

Why am I writing about these play activities and calling them vacations? These short interludes of play between the unending list of chores made life on the farm more bearable—even enjoyable. My grandfather was often heard saying, "All work and no play makes Jack a dull boy." He also said, "Work first, then play." This was the combination that led to a balanced upbringing. The right balance of work and play makes a person more productive in their job. As a business leader, I learned that having fun as a staff builds a strong work team that is more successful in whatever it does. Rewarding a significant accomplishment with a tangible gift, a "new toy," is more often appreciated than money, which usually gets spent on groceries or paying utility bills. Soccer in the farmyard and other vacations taught me these lessons.

I do remember a couple of *real* vacations, however. These vacations were not trips to Florida or to New York. They were visits to some of my mother's relatives. My mother had a brother who lived in Sudbury. He worked in the nickel mines as a foreman. Our overnight trip to see Uncle Roy and Aunt Irene was special because, as kids, we got to go mountain climbing. This mountain climbing consisted of scrambling up a big rock pile that stood behind their house. As a boy, this hill looked really high, but it was really only a hundred metres or so tall. Somehow, this was a big adventure for a young boy. When it was a couple of days away, visiting Uncle Roy seemed as big as a trip to Hawaii. I don't know why that was the case, but I think it had a lot to do with the fact that those days were so completely new and different from our normal life and surroundings. It was interesting to see how much my dad enjoyed the trip to Sudbury, but it was even more interesting to see how eager he was to get back to the farm. Truly, there is no place like home.

I don't feel deprived because I did not have traditional or novel holidays. When I think about the fun on the farm, extended family showing up for Sunday dinner, baseball games in the pasture field with my cousins, or those Sunday afternoon naps after a hard week of work, I'm convinced that I had the vacation of a lifetime!

CHURCH

When I think about my life as a boy and young man on our farm, I think that some of the most important lessons for me were taught in the areas of faith, religion, and spirituality. The lessons were taught formally and informally, intentionally and by example. All the experiences and lessons have had a huge influence on the area of spirituality in my adult life.

For as long as I can remember, church activities and practices were an important part of my world. We attended church almost every Sunday. I cannot remember any time that I was not eager to attend Sunday school and church. Even on a Sunday, chores had to be done and cows had to be milked, fed, and cared for. There was probably a bit less attention to detail because of the need to get to Sunday school by ten o'clock, but we got it done. I enjoyed going to Sunday school and eagerly looked forward to the classes, where I won awards for Bible verse memorization. Attending the church service was more boring, but there were cousins and friends there. Ours was a small country evangelical church, with about one hundred people who called Burford Baptist Church their home.

Burford Baptist Church was not always the church we attended. The whole MacKenzie family, including my grandparents and extended family, attended Mount Vernon Community Church. It was a small white country church that sat on a hill in the hamlet of Mount Vernon. Our family attended this church because it sat near the farms where our family worked. This church was the social heart of the local farm community, with church suppers, quilting clubs, and bingo nights. The churchyard was filled with the tombstones of church members who had passed way over the years. My parents are buried there.

I write about this little church because it has taught me one of my first and most important lessons about faith and spirituality. My dad was very involved in leadership in this church. As it turned out, a new minister came to be the pastor of the church. I don't remember all the details, but I vaguely recall that there were teachings from this minister that my father struggled with. He couldn't balance what he understood as Biblical teachings with the sermons he heard from the minister. I remember his struggle with how to deal with this issue. After much mental anguish, Dad chose to stop attending this church, a church that he grew up in, a church that his friends attended. He moved our family to the Baptist church I referred to earlier. I know nothing about the basis for the big decision my father made. What I do know is that my dad's faith and beliefs were so important to him that he was prepared to make such a significant decision, which impacted the entire family. This experience, which I observed as a young boy, had a very profound effect on me. If my dad did what he did, I concluded that matters of faith, belief, and practice must be very, important. This experience has influenced my decisions about my beliefs and has caused me to do my own thinking with respect to my faith and practice.

This lesson lay dormant in me for many years. As a teenager, I was subjected to a rigid, legalistic kind of religious training. I didn't take the time to really try to understand what I was being taught. As a teenager, my friends, sports, and fun were important. Thinking about theology was the furthest thing from my mind. As an adult, I think my faith could have been summed up by the sentence, "Don't drink, smoke, swear, chew, or date any girls that do."

Even though we attended a conservative church with its list of rules and regulations, there was a marked difference between my mother and my dad with respect to adherence to the "list." Mom was eager for us to have a daily family devotion time, whereas Dad was indifferent. He went along with Mom because he respected her perspective and approach to her faith practices, but she was the one who led these painful sessions of a Scripture reading, prayer time, and life lessons. The frequency of "family worship," as it was called, would ebb and flow based on the busyness of the farm activities. Mom was a strong but quiet spiritual leader in our family. We boys would quietly chafe and squirm under her views and admonishments. However, as adults we all knew that she prayed for the family. Mom prayed for her children, grandchildren, and great-grandchildren daily, right up until her death. From her, I learned that I need to live what I believe.

My mother's strong legalistic views made me start thinking about the inconsistencies I saw in the teachings and rules. I began to wonder how this "God of love" could come across as so mean. A classic example occurred in my twelfth grade. Our high school was small. My class had five students in it. One of my classmates planned a year-end day at the lake to celebrate the end of our high school careers. We planned to go to Lake Erie to spend the afternoon on the beach, with swimming and a barbeque. This event was scheduled for a Sunday. Mom, with a heavy sarcastic sigh, said, "Well, if you think you can go to that event and still keep God happy, then go ahead." What pressure I felt! Both Mom and God on my case.

After a mental struggle, the day at the beach won out. I even managed to enjoy myself! Looking back on this event, I realize that it was an important time in my life, as I began to get a glimmer of the inconsistencies in so much of religion. I began to believe that there were a couple of core issues that were foundational to understanding spirituality, and that much of the other teachings were designed to keep people under control and full of guilt. It took me a long time to fully shed this sense of guilt and the need to "keep God happy." I'm glad to be free of that religious prison.

My dad, a quiet man who never said much, was a man who held simple, deep beliefs as far as his faith and practice were concerned. His kind of faith and spirituality were characterized by acts of generosity, kindness, and integrity. He attended church regularly with the family, enjoyed the social activities that were part of church life, and took his turn in leadership. He understood his faith in simple terms. He believed that God loved all of humanity, including him, and that it wasn't his job to make any distinctions between denominations, sects, or other expressions of faith and practice. Yes, Dad was a quiet man and rarely reacted to my mom's more rigid views about religious activity. One incident defines his understanding of spirituality.

Dad loved to play Rook, a popular card game which involved bidding how many points you could make in a hand. It has its own deck of cards. He was a good player. One Sunday afternoon, my dad, my uncle Tom, my cousin, and I were enjoying a lively game of Rook. Mom appeared in the room and confronted Dad.

"Do you guys think you should be playing Rook? It's Sunday."

Dad calmly looked at my mother and quietly responded, "Ruth, when we get to Heaven, I'll answer for Rook. You answer for Scrabble."

Mom turned on her heel and, without another word, left the room. Rook—and when it was okay to play the game—was never mentioned again. In fact, that Christmas, we all received a set of Rook cards from Mom. Point made!

My father's understanding and perspective about faith and practice is illustrated by a conversation I had with him when I was a teenager. I mentioned earlier that my dad lived his adult life with the effects of polio on his body.

One day, I asked, "Dad, did you every ask God to heal you?"

"Oh, yes," he said. "I have been healed. I wasn't cured, but I have been healed." He explained this distinction further. "Healing," he said, "is the place in your life where you have the best understanding of the overwhelming love of God and the Creator's full delight in you. Yes, I have been healed."

Mom and Dad were both strong and significant influences on my views of, and thoughts about, spirituality. However, the lessons I learned from my grandfather are the ones that have influenced me most profoundly. Grandpa was the poster boy of a quiet, stoic Scotsman. He never said much about any topic, whether it was politics, the weather, sports, or news from the town. So, when my grandfather spoke, it meant something.

Grandpa had a deep relationship with the land. I believe that his Scottish and Celtic heritage deeply affected his life. Celtic Christianity is an ancient form of the Christian faith that places a large emphasis on the importance of nature and how it connects us to the Creator. Simply put, God is displayed in nature. Our relationship to nature and our respect for nature reveals our understanding of, and relationship to, God.

This was how my grandfather's spirituality was revealed. You had to pay attention. He would kneel on the soil, dig a bit in the dirt, looking for the germinating seeds, and say, "God provided that seed with everything it needs." That would be it. No more words.

On another occasion, I was helping him with the delivery of a calf with a cow who was having some trouble on her own. We pulled the calf, wiped the afterbirth off it, and sat back watching the cow nuzzle the calf and lick it. The calf would struggle to its feet and then, on wobbly legs, look for its first meal. With a satisfied look, full of wonder, Grandpa would quietly remark, "Aye, laddie. God has it right. It's a wonderful Creation we've been given. Let's take good care of it!"

These lessons remain with me. When I see an eagle soar; when I watch my dog romp; when I see flowers bloom; when the humming-bird harvests nectar from a blossom, I see the Creator, God.

A Celtic teacher says, "I read the Creation story when God declared that His Creation was good and that humankind was very good. I also read the end of the book. His mind never changed." That was my grandfather's spirituality.

The only way I can sum up these lessons from my upbringing is to share with you the verses from the Christian Scriptures that were the words that my dad lived by.

Micah 6:8 says:

"This is what God asks of you, only this....

To act justly,

To love mercy, and

To walk humbly with your God."

FINAL THOUGHTS

Writing these few brief stories and experiences has moved me. My mind has been taken back, with gratefulness, to the days and years of my life in Burford, on Elgar Lane Farm. I know that everyone has a unique life story and journey. I now understand that my story and my life have been unquestioningly influenced by the people, the events, and the circumstances that I experienced. It doesn't make my story special, but it is mine. My story has moulded my thinking, my attitudes, and my perspective about my world. My desire for you is that you realize and understand that the story you are in is your story, too.

Enjoy it! Celebrate it! Learn from it!

I struggle to summarize the totality of the lessons I learned "over the rail fence" on the farm. I learned generosity, kindness, loyalty, integrity, and stewardship, just to name a few.

I think that all these lessons can be summarized in the words of Grandpa: "Remember that the most important thing you have is your name. You are a MacKenzie. Protect it! Defend it! Live what it means!"

PHOTOS

THE FARM

The farm -1949

The farm - Winter 1949

Winter on the farm

The farm in 1979

Big red barns

EARLY DAYS

Grandpa Mackenzie, age 18, 1909

Grandpa MacKenzie, 1911

THE ANIMALS

Mare with foal

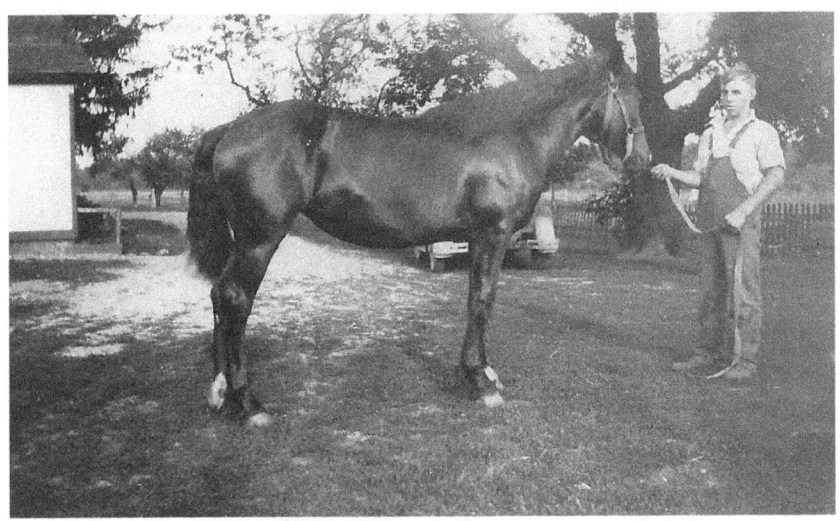

Dad with his horse, Jim

Grandpa with his team, ready to work

Dad with his team of horses

Grandpa with his prize-winning horse

A champion Guernsey bull

Ready for the show ring

Three beautiful horses

Dad and his friend with a colt

Dad at age 21, before polio, ready to work

Planting the crop

Cutting the crop

"Stooking" the grain

Plowing the garden

Spreading "fertilizer"

Off to church in the winter

Our first tractor

MY FAMILY

Mom and Dad on their wedding day, September 13, 1947

Mom and Grandpa MacKenzie

Mom, Grandpa, and Laddie

Dad and Grandpa

Grandpa Mackenzie and me at 4 months

Grandpa and Grandma and me at 5 months

Dad and me at 5 months

Grandpa, Grandma and me at 6 months

Grandpa Mackenzie, Grandpa Day and me at 8 months

Mom and me at 15 months

Grandpa and me on a hayride

Dad and me, age 2

Giving Murray a toboggan ride

Mom and her boys with 'Blackie'

Hockey on the pond, Ken age 14, Jim age 10, Murray age 3

Summer on the farm, age 15

Ready for University, age 18

CPSIA information can be obtained
at www.ICGtesting.com
Printed in the USA
BVHW032337120721
611802BV00001B/1